DISCARD

The Muscled Truce

THE MUSCLED TRUCE

p o e m s

Catharine Savage Brosman

Louisiana State)|(University Press
Baton Rouge
2003

Designer: Amanda McDonald Scallan
Typeface: Sabon, Optima display
Printer and binder: Thomson-Shore, Inc.

Library of Congress Cataloging-in-Publication Data:

Brosman, Catharine Savage, 1934–
   The muscled truce : poems / Catharine Savage Brosman.
      p. cm.
   ISBN 0-8071-2889-9 (alk. paper) — ISBN 0-8071-2890-2 (pbk. : alk. paper)
   I. Title.
   PS3552.R666M87 2003
   811'.54—dc21

                                                    2003007303

The paper in this book meets the guidelines for permanence and durability of the Committee on Pro-
duction Guidelines for Book Longevity of the Council on Library Resources. ⊚

Grateful acknowledgment is made to the editors of the following publications, in which some of the
poems herein first appeared: *Anglican Theological Review:* "Painting, Anonymous, circa 1700"; *Autumn
Harvest: A Collection of Modern Poetry,* edited by John H. Morgan (Bristol, Ind.: Quill Books, 2001):
"Shadows"; *The Classical Outlook:* "King Minos Speaks"; *Critical Quarterly:* "In the Patio," "On the
Lake Fork of the Gunnison"; *Chronicles: A Magazine of American Culture:* "At Saqqara," "In the San
Juans," "On Prytania Street: Tending Lafayette Number 1," "Sweet Olive," "Syzygy"; *Edge City Re-
view:* "Up Island"; *Image: A Journal of Religion and the Arts:* "Bells in Guanajuato"; *Louisiana Litera-
ture:* "In the Virgin Islands"; *Sewanee Review:* "At the Lawrence Memorial," "Byron Leaves England
for the Last Time, 1816," "From a Letter of Queen Victoria before the Wedding of the Princess Royal,"
"Inner Music," "René Char Leaves France, 1944," "Thomas Coryate in India"; *Smartish Pace:* "Pigeon
Man," "The Young Bird"; *South Carolina Review:* "Carolina," "Darby House" "Ernst Hanfstaengl in
England," "Near the Gers"; *Southern Review:* "On Her Sixty-Sixth Birthday," "Robins," "Sunset."
Eleven of the poems in section II, "The Muscled Truce," were published in a chapbook, *The Swimmer
and Other Poems* (Edgewood, Ky.: R. L. Barth, 2000); "The Skater" was inscribed as a holograph poem
in twenty-five copies of that booklet.

CONTENTS

"Il n'y a pas d'amour de vivre sans désespoir de vivre."
[There is no love of life without despair of life.]
—CAMUS, *L'Envers et l'endroit*

1 → A DISTANT SHORE

King Minos Speaks

That bull-boy was an awful nuisance—dreadfully
embarrassing as well—until I hired Daedalus
to build the labyrinth, and left him there.
It was not cruelty; the creature has all luxuries—
perfumes and baths and servants—plus the freshest
offerings, with their tender flesh. How foolish
women are: she could have chosen here,
among my courtiers—handsome, some of them,

well bred, intelligent; but no—it had to be a bull.
The fault of old Poseidon, to be sure, that meddling
god turned spiteful when I would not sacrifice
the animal. I should have acquiesced, agreed
to slaughter him with art and ceremony, as befits
fertility, and scatter virile blood and seed
upon the sea.—And so Pasiphaë became the talk
of all the palace. I renounced her—you can

understand. A silly fate, ignoble—insignificant,
withal: there must be other women.—I have heard
of one Athenian so bold as to proclaim that he
will slay the Minotaur and free his city
from its tribute. That, now, is another matter,
when my royal pride is staked, and too the welfare
of this island. Surely he will not prevail—a youth,
a foreigner. And yet I feel disaster: Icarus

is never distant from my mind; I saw him fall,
the melted wax a vapor in the sun, the wings
detached, his body feeble as a reed. True, I am
the son of Zeus—a king, and powerful. But so
are gods, and force intoxicates, as that narcotic
wafts along the labyrinth to keep the monster
calm; I fear their jealousy. Crete was once
a dream of stone. It will not last, since nothing

lasts: we all are friable; the palace walls, despite
my workers, crack, like faces of old men.
A thousand years from now, what will men know?
I give them my advice: to watch their wives,
their daughters. Ariadne shows a streak
of independence, making eyes at youths who hang
around the beaches, trying to insinuate herself
with guardians of the maze. In a secret chamber

lie my wealth and, in four scripts, the tablets
of my wisdom. Keen is he who will unseal
them and retrieve the key. I shall be dead, after
much suffering perhaps, which purifies;
then what we did will dazzle those who dig
the eddying sands in the confusions of another
world, while waters crash from sea-caves,
trumpeting, and chariots gather on a crimson shore.

At Saqqara

He felt the threads of faith unraveling—
his mind a wilderness, his bones a bit
of mineral—and all his body shook
as if possessed. He took the alphabet,
undid it, twisted it into a code,
and wrote in cryptic letters on the stone:
"Now in the name of God before all things,

remember me, the poor and humble man.—
I, Victor." Thus he carved—a flake, a chip,
the stylus scratching in the darkness. Bells
tolled ominously in the cloister; prayers
fell heavy as a judgment, echoing
beyond the walls. He watched. Along the dunes,
enigmas in a windy tongue appeared

at morning, shifted, changed again by night.
He read his doom and left the secret words
as part of time, then saw his life run out
where alpha and omega met again—
beseeching passersby to read his name
when dervish winds go whirling in the sky,
and pestilential suns redeem the world.

Thomas Coryate in India

To his, my travels are as nothing. Europe,
first—or much of it, at least
(which I have likewise seen, but mostly
not on foot). Back in Somerset,
he visited remembrance again
through words, his Jacobean English
flavored by the spice of foreign phrases
and his macaronic Latin. Then
he left for Asia Minor and the Holy Land—
Jerusalem, Aleppo—passed the old

Euphrates and the Tigris, got to Persia,
finally walking 2700 miles to India beside
a caravan. Along that route
he spent, he claimed, just three pounds
sterling—counting being cozened out
of several shillings by some Christians
in Armenia. He found, beyond
the Indus, British enclaves—factors, traders,
strange expatriates, a chaplain,
and an embassy, a bit itinerant. Ajmer,

Hardwar, Kangra, and Mandu: he turned up
everywhere, alone, at court—a friend
of sorts to the ambassador, distributing
his wit, petitioning the Moghul,
making his hundred-rupee gift go far,
in distance and in mind. What is the sense
of life, if not to use it, risk it—writing
with the body on the world, feet and hands
and eyes as styluses of passion?
Time, for him, was multiplied by tongues,

horizons, visions, in his trekking
over dunes of schist or by the riverbanks,
their mud flats wrinkled in the sun.
Like shoes he left behind, hung up,
he wore his soul until the light shone through.
Perhaps, at Surat, where he died,
among its great stone walls that draw
the sea to frenzy and the gardens
drunk on carmine fruit, he wept
for Somerset, the combes and hills

and hedgerows, or his father's rectory,
while from his belly ran the last
of all the life he had digested. Even so,
the tomb where, legend said, he lay
did not contain him, surely: neither
monument nor house of bones can hold
desire, which rides on hot and oceanic
winds that strafe the palm trees
day and night, and waves of undulating sand,
immense, and rippling with mirage.

Byron Leaves England for the Last Time, 1816

My poetry comes easily as breath—
a canto in a week when words flow fast
and drink is good to me. And women, too,
some paid for, to be sure, and some diseased,
but others freely, of high rank, who fall
for love like ripened, almost rotten, fruit—
my sister even . . . Boys and men as well,
although a voice from Cambridge drove me mad

with fear, and I left England. Back again,
I wanted Annabella; Caroline
desired me; Augusta, still in heat,
was there like poison; Claire was next, and bears
within her womb the evidence. The law
is sniffing at my ankles—sodomy
and incest smelling foul; my money's gone,
perhaps my brain. But not my art! It holds

them all, despite their scorn, and they will see
me honored yet. The foolish reader thinks
that Harold, Conrad, Lara are myself;
though all are creatures of me, none is I.
I draw upon the public flesh, and write
perversion on the body they disguise:
my violence is theirs, my lust—my foot,
their visible deformity. If men

suppose that evil will succumb to good
by rational arrangement, they are wrong;
it merely will invent itself again
or settle in the gaol of the mind.
And so, I'm off to sea: "Once more upon
the waters, and once more!" There will be whores
and sailors, countesses and poetry,
and deaths in Italy, and deaths in Greece;

and I shall make my reputation stand
for freedom—not that I believe in it,
nor anything except myself: but *that,*
I shall secure by gestures and by words,
and grave my name and image into time
and England's conscience. So farewell, my loves,
my hypocrites; you will remember me,
a blazing star that burnt itself to ash.

From a Letter of Queen Victoria before the Wedding of the Princess Royal

Windsor, 1858

. . . So that, although I must be pleased, I still
shall tremble for her, for myself. To be
a girl so recently, and now be thrust
to womanhood! The marriage rite, for all
its flowers, lace, and ceremonial joy,
resembles more a sacrifice, with her
the willing lamb.—I do not understand
the ways of the Creator for our sex—

desired by men, and yet in servitude;
nor can I quite approve the means ordained
to have a child—such impropriety,
and such a long ordeal! To wish on her
this "happiness," as it is called, may be
to wish her death.—Of course I love my dear,
my chosen Albert; and my children too
I cherish, whom he fathered for me; yet,

he is a man . . . Nor can we ascertain
that Vicky's lot will be so fortunate
as mine.—When I was marrying, did I
reflect this way? I did not even know
my innocence! A mother later turns
enlightened eyes on those she suffered for,
and on the past. At least I have the hope
that Prussia, in the person of her prince

and English princess, may remain our friend
forever. When I think of all the blood,
the senseless suffering at Sebastopol,
I want no more of war. Not that I wished
for it before! And yet it came. The next
could well be worse. Their future heir and prince,
and all the court, will surely help us keep
the peace of Europe. What a burden!—Now

8

I must control myself, and say that all
is well if God should will it.—Comfort me,
my dear; for when the celebration ends
and they are gone, her absence will consume
me, as by cold.— I thought once, in a dream,
I saw a figure with a withered arm,
who moved among the shadows on a field
of mutilated forms and ghostly trees;

and men rose up to curse him from their graves.
But what has this to do with us?—A dread,
a premonition for our race.—I beg
you, pardon these extravagances. Be
of cheer: we have no other means to live,
nor love. The wedding day, I shall be clad
in silk and diamonds, and shall not shed
a tear. Till then, good-bye. Victoria R.

Carolina

South Carolina, 1875

They found us drifting in the sea, along
the coast—the rations almost gone, the three
of us half crazy from the wind and sun,
the boat a little leaky, but afloat.
From Saint-Domingue, the currents had been strong,
the weather fair; we had been carried up
past Charleston, we were told. I don't recall

the journey well, you know—at five, bereft
(how much I did not realize then) of both
my parents, sailing empty seas with Lou,
our old *négresse*, and Georges, my brother. She
had learned (it was the years of those revolts
of Haitians under Toussaint L'Ouverture)
that all the servants and the slaves—herself

included—were to rise against the French
that week and slaughter everyone. She would
not do it to us—children she had nursed
and loved; and yet she could not speak against
her people. She had thought to take us out—
a boating party, so she said. She'd heard
of islands thick with traveler's palm, where birds

refreshed themselves in flight. We left, the sails
like angels' wings. She'd managed to purloin
a few supplies—fresh water most of all,
some food, some sheets. We lived on coconuts,
I think, and sugar, toward the last; she may
have had some rum. She sang to us at night
her Creole lullabies. When we were saved,

she told our story in her broken French.
The strange thing is, it was some French
who found us—Huguenots. And stranger still,
my name is Caroline, as if somehow
by Providence my mother had foreseen
our odyssey. — Now Lou, good woman, lies
in Carolina ground. We had, of course,

no photographs; my parents' smiles became
a phosphorescent sea, translucent, dark,
untouchable—a ghostly imago
receding in the waves. Yet now they seem
like children, younger than my own; they walk
beneath the palm trees in my dreams and laugh,
the trade winds scattering perfume, or sit

at sunset, holding hands, and speak of France
and golden journeys. Look, the tide is high . . .
sargasso shines in jeweled light. At dusk,
I listen to the birds that wheel and dive,
and watch the stars grow powdery and dense—
and sometimes think I hear a song, a shout,
two shadows calling on a distant shore.

Darby House

Iberia Parish, Louisiana, 1875

This silence stifles me, a chain, a cell
of my design. It stood for punishment—
but who has been chastised? For seven years
I have not spoken to a soul within
this house: we've had no servants since the war,
when we lost nearly everything save life;
no children; just the centenary oaks,
a place half-ruined, brothers, sister. Worlds

ago, we were in Paris, he and I,
two Creoles from la Nouvelle-Orléans,
received in the salons, attending plays
by Dumas and Labiche, or the ballet
or concerts, strolling on the boulevards
and by the Seine, its bridges shining gold
like bracelets in the sunset; we were shown
the Palace of the Tuileries, now turned

to cinders by the Communards; I even met
the Emperor at court, and Eugénie,
his Spanish jewel. Perhaps it was not right
—our fortune, built on others' laboring,
and not by choice. But who can choose
his station? Were they not well fed and free
to live, if not to leave?—while now
they are the darlings of the North,

and free to rot and die in slums. And were
those Yankees saints, who murdered, robbed, and burnt—
the mercenaries of ill-gotten wealth
who fought for railroad barons, bankers, thieves,
for oil of whales tormented, sailors' lives?
When all was gone but Darby, we came back,
sold off the land, retired to the house
to live (I thought) with honor in defeat,

like François Premier, a prisoner,
who mourned to see his squire manacled
behind his horse, but mutely turned aside
when *he* was mocked. My brother had in mind
another model—Yankee: business deals
with carpetbaggers; I refused, and shall
eat dirt, if necessary.— It is time
to write this down; the years are not so young,

and Darby too will be a derelict
one day, the garden gone to seed, the wind
its ghost. So be it: we cannot redeem
ourselves, nor change the way the world returns
as counterfeit our deeds—iniquity
or good. I'll walk out to the gallery;
the sky seems lighter now, as if my words
of testimony had released a weight,

or brought an airy premise. If I die
before the others, may they know what pride
has done for them: we all are relics, but
my name is good. I'll hold my peace; by now
it is our custom; yet perhaps I'll smile
tonight when lamplight, searching, draws my face
out of the darkness, and their voices drift
and fade to phantom memories in the trees.

René Char Leaves France, 1944
Southern France

The captive springtime moves on espadrilles
among mimosas flaming into bloom,
their coral lamps illumined through the hills,
investing the Vaucluse with their perfume.

With others, René Char awaits the news
from England, knowing that the final fight
is coming. Orders meanwhile. To refuse
all compromise has been his word. Tonight

he's flying out for Africa, above
the olive groves and lemon-scented earth
to which his acts are rooted, as in love,
inscribing him, beyond the fact of birth,

by poetry and sacrifice for France.
He leaves in secrecy: no fanfares yet;
but down the darkened slopes of the Durance,
where stealthily the shadows cast their net,

his men have lighted fires in farewell,
whose constellations shine along his route
as brilliant sea-marks in the mistral's swell—
each star fraternal and a last salute.

Ernst Hanfstaengl in England

London, 1945

It all began in nineteen-nineteen. War,
for some of us at least, had signified
ideal and honor—awful as it was,
four years of suffering and massacre
in fields that never have recovered. *Ja.*
It was the treaties, though, that ruined us.
They turned us into beaten dogs, half-starved

and left to feed on words. Enraged, I bought
them, like my fellow officers—believed
that empire and the Wilhelmine idea
could be restored. I was a fool. Before
the Munich *Putsch,* I met with Hitler, gave
advice, became a follower. A *fool,*
I said. In thirty-three, he sought me out

again. He liked his thugs, but *Junkers* too
were useful. Sometimes he would listen—mad,
but strangely rational.—If I'd been there
last summer, I'd have thought in time about
that table . . . After war broke out in Spain
der Führer sent me on a mission (so
he said); my orders were to be unsealed

in flight. It was a trap; I had become
too critical. The pilot was to drop
me—push me out—without a parachute.
"An accident" would be announced. The day
turned stormy, though; a rage of snowflakes clawed
around us, and we eddied in the wind.
We had to land. The *Schwarzwald* lay below

15

us, but the pilot found a clearing. Then
he told me. We were both at risk, since he
had failed, and wrecked the plane, and I was dead
in principle. He fled toward Freiburg, where,
he said, he had a brother; whether he
arrived I did not learn. I hid at first,
then moved at nighttime, following the streams,

and found the Rhine. I never shall return.
Among the burning ruins and the camps,
the old ideals have died, and won't revive;
ten million corpses rot around the earth,
fanatics rule in Russia, France is still
corrupt, and torture has become a means
of politics. I've done for England what

I could; thank God for England. Spring has come
with victory; it gambols, shouts, and plays
among the tattered gardens of the mews,
and on the downs the clouds meander, mild
and free above the whorls of sheep. I'll go
to Sussex, make my peace with time,
and watch the battered ships of war wing home.

Near the Gers

Southwest France, 1950

She thought it was a bit of Moorish blood—
a Spanish ancestor—that made my skin
so dark. And yet my eyes are harebell blue,
you note. But here, I must relate it all
in order.—So, the maharajah's son
was sent to school in England. He seduced
the daughter of a duke, who packed her off
to France (still civilized, but far enough

away) to bear the child. From India,
the maharajah settled on the girl
some eighty thousand pounds. She then returned
to Britain, and presumably lived well
on such a fortune. Nothing can be known
of her—the name, the county, *nothing*. That
was in the bargain—anonymity.
The boy she left behind was I. I think

of her, and try to conjure up a face
unseen, imagining her honeyed hair,
her fragile eyes, her figure growing full—
alone, and exiled to the continent
on pretext of a journey. How it all
was managed I don't know; but at my birth
I was presented as another's child,
a woman who had not been told her own

had died. She never learned the truth; nor I,
until . . . My father *only* knew. They left
their being in my trust; I was their son,
if we are what the world believes. She died
when I was twenty; Father lived for ten
more years, his own survivor. At the last,
—his voice like murmuring water under moss—
he told his secret, having sheltered me,

17

two women—and perhaps himself so long.
The worst thing was, I had a fiancée.
I thanked him like an automaton, went
outside, and walked across the summer wheat
to reach the valley of the Gers, beyond
that line of trees. The earth seemed alien,
as if its features had dissolved, and I
a lunatic who does not recognize

his name. A path cuts steeply down along
the river; as I ran, the willows stung
my face, and once I slipped on spongy soil
and fell. I did not want to drown, but *find*
myself among those dense and foreign signs.
I could not bear to tell the girl I loved,
—her family would not have understood—
nor marry her in falsehood. That explains

why I'm alone. They are long dead, I think,
the maharajah's heir, the English girl,
and I am seventy—an accident,
a man and an enigma. Are we all
in exile from ourselves? —Perhaps you'd like
to stay outdoors; we'll have our cocktails here,
al fresco, looking at a prism of fields,
and late, impassioned measures of the light.

Inner Music

New Orleans, 1975

After interrogation and a long
and miserable march, my arm in shreds,
the VC separated us—the four
Americans shot down and found along
that sector. I was beaten, then removed
to solitary, where the visions flashed

again—the fire and crash, the jungle men
disguised as trees and shouting. What they left
me—taking everything of use and things
they knew I wanted—was immobile time,
without the possibilities to act
that give time meaning, and my body's pained

resistance, with its streams of memory,
the stones with which I shaped the landscapes where—
the reader of the world—I was the wind
that seared the desert, or the winter sun
exhausted from its ash; where from the past
emerged its words: a poem's wit, the voice

of my desire, and her woman's way
of answering. Surprised by foreign speech
recalled, I listened, practiced, dredged again,
and dreamt in French. I painted in the dark
imaginary canvases, their mist
releasing light, as in the late Monets,

conceived in desperate love. Like Homer, blind,
who told of Hector, I remembered those
unburied, fallen this time to a cause
that few would sing; I thought of Beethoven,
and heard, alone, a silent music. When
deliverance came, I flew back to the States

a thinner man by thirty pounds. Beyond
the mangled arm, the throbbing cage of dreams,
and those denouncing us, remain to bloom
the magic lilies, purple in the sun,
as waves of inner music reach the shore
and break to join the full, majestic sound.

Up Island
Victoria, B.C., 1980

He pleaded, cursed, cajoled; she would not change
her mind. He told her love had *chosen him*
(the war, the missions flown across the Rhine
day after day, the fear of death that clutched
his belly, then that Yorkshire girl and war
forgotten for a moment in her arms).
"But *you*," my mother said, "had made a choice
already—me, these children. No divorce."

He was a dour man, but in his rage
(I still remember) roared—a lion trapped—
his Scottish blood on fire. Still, she did
not yield. Some residue of decency
prevented him from killing us; he thought
instead of long-term vengeance.—Yes: we moved
up island, leaving everything behind—
the house, our lives. He bought some land. We slept

in tents at first, then built a cabin, log
by log—a penance for us all. I walked
to school, ashamed to be a city girl
in dresses, when the others were in flannel shirts
and jeans. The boys stayed back and worked. We had
no water in the house, no light but oil;
I did my lessons on a slate. It snowed
quite heavily that spring, and gales blew in

between the chinks; my father had to hike
four miles across the drifts to get supplies.
One Christmas later, we contrived—the boys
and I—to buy a gift for her; I chose
a nightgown, wrapped it, put it on her bed.
She thought a moment that it was from *him*;
her eyes were radiant. When she understood,
the weir of self-control gave way to tears.

You see now why my brothers left: first Dan,
the elder, gone one day, then James. I stayed
and finished school. The university
became my dream.—The letter said I was
admitted; Father tore it up, and soon
he packed me off to work. My mother died,
and after that I sent no money home.
You'll notice on this canvas: past the woods

there was a railroad trestle, and a road
that loggers used; I vary them each time
I paint them, going back (I cannot help
myself), but seeing them in different lights,
the girders almost disappearing in the sun,
or shadowy with storm. The aspen shone
like that, in fall, ideas of gold among
the firs.—From James? We never heard. But Dan—

he got away in time, thank God. He lives
in Manitoba, half a continent
away. Neuroses are a gift; they've let
me paint. I'm going to do the river next,
unleashed along its stony bed, the way
my mother wept. One day I'll paint the moors,
the bracken thick and wet, the heather dark,
a lonely woman moaning to the wind.

At the Lawrence Memorial

I am strangely moved,
given that I do not like him much,
certainly am no idolater. Is it the climb
from San Cristóbal up to Lobo Mountain—
those thousand feet or more
of rise in second gear along five miles
of gravel roads, through sagebrush,
piñon and scrub oak, then, higher,

yellow pine—the ponderosa—full
and phallic? Should I say
it is the famous Taos light, perhaps
the solitude—I the only visitor this day,
finding no one on the ranch except
two horses, nuzzling each other
in a pool beneath the trees? Is it the birds,
who whistle in antiphony

as if to welcome me into their sanctum,
into Lawrence's—and, too,
the phoenix rising still (as Frieda wished)
above the altar where his ashes
are commingled with the gravel
of New Mexico in rough cement? Is it
instead the evidence of love,
or else what passed for it—three women,

rivals for his favor, beyond death,
with the Italian lover, and D.H., in combat
for his soul through others,
mediators to the inner man? Their passion
becomes palpable—a texture
where the air is caught, a muffled moan
that takes on resonance,
and desire thick and sweet as resin. Or

is it, finally, the art which lasts,
perverted, disputatious, and offensive,
but still art . . . ?—Reluctantly, I leave,
feeling how the past divides
from me—an enemy, alive. Descending,
I devour the vision westward—
stratus clouds in morning hues
topping the cumulus, and the aromatic,

undulating desert, reaching to the river
gorge and native lands. Peace, Lorenzo,
to us all, the dead, the living,
despite everything—even
the disordered pleasure that for you
was life itself; peace, since words
endure, the mind consumed still slowly
seeping out—green, mineral, and cool.

The Beekeeper

In linen, hat, and gauze
she tends the humming hives,
a vigil without pause
around the honeyed lives.

A sting from time to time
reminds her of the bite
of love, which is a mime,
and shimmers in the light,

but shoots a poisoned dart—
and how the sweetest care
—a jewel, a tender heart—
can turn into a snare.

And so she meditates,
mellifluous, refined,
on memories of fetes,
still golden in her mind;

and when the autumn brings
its chills and idle hours,
she sweeps up brittle wings
and lives on garnered flowers.

The Gardener

To wait on sun and rain,
as heaven may propose;
to order his demesne,
or worry for a rose,

a man abandons time—
the trope of days and hours—
like poets for a rhyme—
or measures it in flowers.

He tends each plant and tree,
pursuing each defect
as if assuming he
were summer's architect;

and under autumn's skies
with pruners, rake, and spade
devises their disguise
for winter's masquerade;

then to the gardener's shed
to leave his tools behind,
and cultivate instead
the garden of his mind.

The Dressmaker

Between the eager eyes
and luncheon, dinner, ball,
she labors to devise
the way a skirt will fall,

a ruffle, yoke, or plait—
the images refined—
and thus to mediate
from beauty in the mind

to sleek and sexy shape,
or tailored suit or dress,
assuring fit and drape
for passing happiness.

She measures, cuts, and seams
along material lines,
but knows that it is dreams
her fantasy designs;

and in the night, the feel
of such a silken ruse
transfigures her ideal
with clothes of tragic muse.

The Golfer

Ascribing to the sport
the seriousness of quest,
he is the classic sort,
whose tee shots are a test;

who looks at every game
as if it were a war,
and universal fame
depended on the score.

His drives bisect the trees,
or if he hits the sand,
he chips his way with ease
to make his final stand,

and, proving on the green
a putter's loving skill,
experiences a keen,
almost erotic thrill;

then, finishing his day,
he turns toward home and wife,
referring to his play
to par the course of life.

The Painter

The world appears quite full,
its properties entire,
and yet she feels the pull
Prometheus felt with fire,

to wrest from earth and heaven
or from her tender heart,
as a fantastic leaven,
epiphanies of art.

With brush and palette knife,
she paints illusion's stuff,
an imitation life,
a dream—and yet enough

to let her realize
by what the gods forbade
that truth may be disguise,
while beauty must be sad,

but she, the medium
of such cathartic trance
that visions can become
the substance of the dance.

The Pianist

The notes convulse the air
before the final pause.
He rises, shakes his hair,
and bows to the applause.

The power of desire
preserved in every chord,
his purpose is entire,
and passion its reward,

for, with his practiced hands
and genius in his ears,
his body understands
all beauty that he hears;

but in another space,
where music is unknown
and evening has no face,
he finds himself alone,

and on the heart's clavier
a silent sound is heard,
the forming of a tear,
the falling of a bird.

The Traveler

She opens up her maps
and dreams of Italy,
Japan, Brazil perhaps,
or the Aegean Sea.

The known or the unseen,
she favors what is far—
anticipation, keen;
the world, her oyster bar.

She knows before the start
that meaning must arise
from what will move her heart—
adventure, love, surprise.

She cannot be deceived:
no matter what they find,
all tourists are relieved
to leave themselves behind,

until they learn the rare
distinction of the game:
the strange is everywhere,
the journey's still the same.

The Camper

The choice is his alone
to rough it in the woods,
without a telephone
and less of worldly goods.

He has his little tent,
his pack and cooking gear,
and thinks his time well spent
if no one else is near.

He cooks the fish he's caught,
he studies plants and birds,
and cultivates his thought,
economizing words,

and even by the fire,
which warms his pensive mood,
forswearing all desire,
believes in solitude.

Yet winds will sing, and trees
will dance, their leaves unfurled,
when in his dreams he sees
connections with the world.

The Hiker

Beside a rocky stream,
past yellow pine and fir,
where sun and shadow dream,
and day belongs to her,

she rises, breathing hard—
impassive, yet intent—
then pauses to regard
her measure of ascent,

before she finds a ledge
to take her higher still,
and scrambles to the edge,
by muscle and sheer will.

Then down the farther side
she follows her surmise,
that steepest trails provide
both view and exercise,

and mountains being fact,
to gaze at or to climb,
their meaning is the act
inscribed in human time.

The Skater

The lake is frozen white;
the trees stand cold and stark.
He skates alone tonight,
a shiver in the dark,

and traces on the ice
the figures of his thought,
composing his device,
infinity and naught—

the zero and the eight
both eloquent and mute,
their immaterial weight
from some celestial chute;

then, gazing at the place
where gods and heroes shine,
correlatives of space,
he cuts a cryptic sign,

that heaven may regard
his momentary flame,
the shadows shaped and starred
for crystalline acclaim.

The Winegrower

The house is moored by pines,
its walls of mellow stone.
Among the laden vines,
she cannot be alone.

With harvest near at hand,
for pinot gris and noir,
she marvels at the land,
admiring its *terroir,*

its undulating slope
and venerable root—
the evidence of hope
that ripens into fruit.

She is a steward here—
the season does the rest;
the wine, another year,
will prove her labor blest,

as bitter grapes ferment
in retrospective eyes,
becoming, by consent,
the vintage of the wise.

The Swimmer

With gestures strong and clean,
he strokes across the pool,
the ambience serene,
the fluid measures cool.

He dips, then swims below,
the surface barely rent—
his motions strangely slow,
the way the light is bent.

Within the buoyant space
his body is confined
by what resists his grace,
yet holds it, as the mind—

a luminous decree,
encountering the shade—
takes purchase on the sea
and cultivates a glade.

He finishes his laps;
his limbs are free and loose—
to move the world, perhaps,
by such a muscled truce.

III ✒ A COSMIC COMEDY

Painting, Anonymous, circa 1700

The skies are tinted mauve and livid green,
and lightning tears the pediment of cloud.
Below, dark figures animate the scene:
three women grieving in a casual crowd.

The middle ground appalls a feeling heart,
but feeds the appetite for blood and pain:
two common thieves hang crucified; apart,
one blameless victim bears the human stain.

At thirty silver coins His head was priced;
He took the kiss, the thornèd crown, the rod.
To some He is a fraud; to us, the Christ.
"So save thyself," they scoff, "if Thou art God."

Around His head the majesty of light
offsets His suffering eyes and silent moan;
some soldiers in the foreground, at the right,
cast lots indifferently with bits of bone

to have His cloak, while hooded figures draw
together toward the left.— The painter's eye
has failed him, though, perhaps from guilt or awe:
the sacred face is blurred, the cloth awry—

as if, a spectator himself, he stood
in tears and helpless in the crowd that poured
their imprecations on the holy rood
and on the broken body of the Lord.

Pigeon Man

On foot, I'm here on Washington, making my way
to Magazine Street and the A&P. Taxis, cars,
and limousines drawn up before Commander's Palace
jam the intersection; valets dash around to open doors;
passels of tourists clog the sidewalks, gaping
at the cemetery gates, ajar, or venturing in, or taking
photographs beside the oak trees. At my back,

the chariots of time have turned to stone. Quick—I leave
the whitened sepulchers and dart between the cars.
On this corner, there's a little gallery, shaded by sweet
olive. Sounds of birds as from Respighi fill
the foliage; inside, cagèd cousins warble; and here's
Pigeon Man in front, holding two birds,
cooing to others at his feet, scattering feed. His hair

is ruffled as the puny feathered creature in his palm;
his chin's unshaven and his look a bit unsettling.
Did Francis also gaze about that way, a hand
outstretched, his inner eye on God? One fancies him
transported here across the centuries, feeling
at home among all our Italians, churches, saints' names
on the streets and parishes. Tonsured, sandal-shod

and girded round by beads, he'd look the part,
but suffer mightily in summer in that frieze. Pigeon
Man wears blue jeans and a faded shirt; he cares
for beauty though (the gallery is his), and doesn't dote
on money much, I think. Cautiously, I step around
his birds, careful not to cast blame with my eyes,
nor yet encourage him to speak. St. Francis too

would be a stranger to me, or St. John the Baptist—
just another New Orleans eccentric with unkempt hair
and visions, passing leaflets out or mumbling
to himself among the tombs—or calling to the crowd
beside Commander's that salvation is at hand.
See, across the river how it comes!—a radiant bird,
through blood-red sun in winged and holy light.

Night Birds

What's this? The blinds were drawn,
the shutters closed, the moon, that lamp
of whimsy, left to lovers—so I thought
at least—and I to Morpheus. But no
indeed! A crack of light, a slim

and enigmatic smile, is flickering
in the darkness of my chamber,
and a jaunty wind, cocking his cap,
whistles at the window, teasing me
from dreams, while on the river a calliope

begins to play. Now the night is filled
with sudden birdsong also. Is it they,
the little finches that I love, red-jacketed
and multi-noted bodies hardly bigger
than a lipstick? How they chatter,

answering each other in their avian
awareness! Yet such little bits
of being! All my limbs seem coarse—
enormous, thick appendages—
and thought a drag, a sticky thread

that spins itself laboriously out. Oh,
dear! I cannot leave it, nor escape
by fluttering, wordless, past the shades
and winging up, nor singing with the birds
in bright, nocturnal antiphons

as the moon provides harmonics: just,
perhaps, invent a beat, a bass line,
resonant upon the body's sounding board,
not delicate, but steady, like the drone
of sleepy monks at matins, mumbling,

chins falling on their chests—common
earth-bound men and ponderous,
but of good will, giving ground to things,
and praising with their rough devotions
all the finer workings of the world.

Bells in Guanajuato

Bells! Bells! Afternoon and evening, *al Atardecer,*
later around ten, again at midnight, matins,
then at seven-ish—not telling, though, the hour
(nineteen rings just now at nine), but, I suppose,
some office or some prayer for the world, for us—in need
as always. Bells around us, in our ears and mind,
like thought—from the church of San Diego,
right across the Jardín de la Unión; bells behind,
in the Basílica Colegiata of Our Lady; Jesuit bells,
in the temple of the Company; Franciscan bells,

a bit more modest, farther on; bells of the templo
de Belén and then San Roque, none quite synchronized
with others. And, when we've counted out the tolling
—fifteen strikes this time—and we believe it's done,
another, then a final ringing resonates, lest we doze off.
Well! We certainly are awake, after having had
day's intimations early. How do the citizens
survive? They must suppress the music, hearing
it inside and unaware, the way you feel your heartbeat
and your breath. Ah, well. An excellent *café*

con leche helps offset the lack of sleep, and then
it's time to visit all these churches from whose carillons
the brassy messages come out. What messages?
That's up to us. We wander through the *callejones,*
stumbling on the paving stones like Proust
and seeing visions. Here is where the loudest bells
must ring, within the butter-colored towers of the basilica.
Look a moment at the pediments and doorways,
all churrigueresques. In the nave, conspicuous art—
gold rivers, solid silver, from the veins just up the hill,

and paintings, gaudy, mannered, and enormous,
with their swooning saints and Christ hung crimson
in his blood; here is a statue, crowned in thorns,
another bent beneath a cross. The altarpiece and cupolas
are huge; I'm dizzy from attempting to embrace
it all. And now the bells begin again about our heads
and everywhere; we do not know ourselves in all this fine
cacophony. So, have we been transported to the heyday
of the Hapsburgs back in Spain, the Viceroys,
the Indians laboring in Valenciana mine, and God above

it all, his jeweled Mother weeping and the martyred
saints with soulful eyes to witness, but the tunnels
dark, the rock resistant, naked shoulders raw
and striped? It is as though their memory were cast
in sound; and if my prayer is not undone, a tinny, tinkling
gong, then let it rise among the votive candles,
through the wisps of incense, ringing out with every
bell of Guanajuato: even we, such strangers
by our time and tongue, are listening, remembering
in our orisons our brethren, burden, and our very souls.

Syzygy

Sun, earth, and moon aligned tonight
in crystal winter cold—first teasing us,
the sun descending in a rose farewell,
the moon in coppery fullness rising
from the river, just beyond the bridges,
hanging for an hour among the lights,
then creeping toward its rendezvous.
The way the soft penumbra lessens

makes me think of time, unnoticed
nearly, till one sees that it is waning;
so the moon appears, as if its edge
were etched by acid, nibbled evenly.
As the silver disk ascends to zenith,
I must circle with it, changing places
at the windows, pivoting, and finally
kneeling by the glass—to see the half-

moon, then a quarter, then a solitary
slice; and I, a poet and a lunar spirit,
frenzied with the spectacle, imagine
how a mortal felt his flesh turn cold
with fright, to see the heavenly lamp
extinguished, as the angels chattered
in anticipation of renascent light. It's
done: Diana is eclipsed. "Come now,"

I beckon to my cat, who does not seem
excited, being a philosopher. "I've had
enough of cosmic comedy. The actors
must be tired. Goodnight! Our minds
are well aligned; our dreams will play
in a proscenium with suns and planets
tumbling on the shadows, juggling stars,
laughing all the way to God's own stage."

Sweet Olive

Walking back from dinner at Commander's Palace
in June's profusion, my English guests have paused
beside the cemetery gate, enchanted at the statuary
and the shadows as they shift among the dwellings
of the dead. Wisps also of my mind home in—bees,

charmed by the honeyed pull of nothingness. Still
roseate, clouds wind-combed to angel hair drift on
downriver, and there is rustling in the oaks—a bird,
a restless limb, a spirit wandering, dreams perhaps,
damp and heavier than breath. A few steps, finally,

a laugh dispel the sorcery. Again we stop, attracted
by perfumes that mingle in the moist and pulsing air
of the Louisiana summer night: the languorous odor
of Cape jasmine in a cypress planter, deadly oleander,
honeysuckle in cascades along a wall of mossy brick,

and then the branches of sweet olive bending down
as if to be admired, their waxen foliage luminous,
their milky blossoms soft and sensual as ringlets
in a Botticelli painting. As we amble on, we talk
of paradise imagined: Persian poetry, the garden

of the Rose, a cloistered fountain with the music
of its arches and the deepest heaven mirrored. Oh,
the feasting of desire on its vision!—wine, ambrosia,
melody, sweet olive by a wall, and a beloved form
embraced. Or will we be as shades more immaterial

than a conceit of figures dancing through the trees
at dawn, like Spanish moss, who vanish in the sun,
or fireflies that flit across sidereal lawns, a moment
visible, then drawn by greater darkness, greater light
of stars yet farther out, still brighter, still unknown?

Sunset

"What a glorious sunset!" say my visitors, as cumulus,
amassed in mesa shapes above the river, glow, striated
pink, vermillion, crimson, crowned with cirrus tinted
gold. "And there—below the bridge—those embers . . .?"
Friends from out-of-town are easily deceived. I must

explain: the sun's gone down *behind* us, flaming. Yes,
we're looking to the West Bank, but we're facing *east*
along the Mississippi's crescent, as a comedy of light
reflected from the Occident is magnified on vapor floes
of rain tomorrow. The spectacle has shifted, sending

shades inside: a bud vase on the table casts a shadow
aureoled in violet, and roses in profusion fill the air
and fall around our feet; our Chardonnay has changed
to Zinfandel. Does evening think it can disguise itself
as dawn? —We gaze, the windows opened. Marbling

appears; a sculptor wind is mining gold remembrances
and shaping for our vesper offerings a Buddha, plump
and enigmatic, on the highest altar. Oh, connections!—
as the world turns round, a vision bridges east and west,
the Buddha smiles to make the old feel young again,

and we are bound to everything—fragments of mineral
ash and drops of rain, ideas drawn out in wisps of cloud,
the children's laughter riffling memory, and a celestial
tumult, brass and cymbals, fading imperceptibly to dusk—
largo, largo, pianissimo, followed by bouquets of stars.

Shadows

In memory of Evelyn Payne

There are such sources to this light—the rose
of summer lengthening to fall, the blue
of trade winds paler now, a sunset pose
reflected on the stones—that shadows too,

aslant along a wall or through the trees,
assume the evening prism. A marine
impression forms like recesses of seas
in mist; the garden ripples, and a green

imagination tints the farthest leaf,
as darker birds of dusk display their wings
a moment, turning at the skyline. Brief,
it is, the world of insubstantial things,

the fragile side of being—but the scene
that correlates our motions, as a glade
gives shape and thought to nothingness, between
the shimmering sunlight and the shifting shade.

The Young Bird

It is nothing: brittle leaves, debris
borne in your palm, one leg—a twig
and tiny foot—broken at the joint,
the other crushed, the body bitten
through, but ombréd indigo intact

along the wingtip—pinnate daysky
turning into dusk. Once, you saw
friends die in fields and foxholes—
mutilated, charred, and screaming
toward their end; you have foreseen

your death—familiar flesh forspent,
manipulated by embalmers —no!
you say, it also shall be burnt; but
for this bird, now honored on a bier
of tissue paper, you have mourned

the more because of its fragility,
its fall—the lightest bit of being
you have loved, the least of breath.
You wrap it in its shroud and show
me what a little thing is life, a toy

to time, yet incommensurate to all
the rest—a moment's warbled note,
a flight of fantasy fulfilling winds,
a flash of blue intention, realized
against indifferent and fiery worlds.

Robins

Strange, it was, on a mountain deck
that looked toward Byers Peak, to peel aside
a mat and gaze down at the robins perching
just below—four hungry, chirping young
ones, nestled on a post, their cherry mouths

agape; from time to time, a parent also,
winging in with insects or a worm. Along
with conversation and the crystal notes of ice
on glass, they made our cocktail music,
grounding us by primal cries. The nest

was rounded as an egg, about to crack.
They showed no fear: to them we were perhaps
phenomena, like thunder, lightning, wind,
and rain, or else were gods—remote, and yet
presiding somehow, cabin stylites,

at the verdant world. Our steps resounded
on the deck a moment; then we settled
into chairs again, refills in hand, while sunset,
spreading crimson from the skyline,
turned our Chardonnay to rose. As if

announcing change, a furious cheeping
followed. The morning afterwards, the birds
were gone; later, in the willows near the creek,
I heard the parents call, and then a rustling
in the grass, and glimpsed a fledgling

trying flight. I thought of mutilated robins
in the past, and birds that froze in rotten leaves,
where I would find them and be wounded
as a girl alone can be—of other bodies, loved,
in stony ground, and light that left

their eyes. My nature shuddered at the dark
necessity of life, that miserable law
of birth and growth—the animal within us
driven to feed in summer's plenitude,
as, prescient, we rehearse for winter's dance.

On the Lake Fork of the Gunnison

Had we bargained for all this? Perhaps—a perfect
campground picketed by spruce, its needled web
so dense that rain at midnight could not penetrate
the sand below; but, on the other hand, the river,
bellowing past, cascading over rocks and fallen
branches, feeding rapids six yards from our feet.
Remembering, I felt its force again—indifferent,
cold, and yet alive, the way it rushed that summer

when my father—young—and I, in hip boots, waded
in among the stones and eddies, casting tenuous
lines for rainbow trout and for ourselves. At night,
this time, its tympani resounded through my sleep;
at dawn, it wakened us with an *aubade,* and kept
us shouting over breakfast; it was there, at noon,
along with lunch, and offered cocktail music, more
a fugue than serenade, at evening. Later, by the fire,

we nodded, drowsy, as the river kept its rhythm;
turning in at ten, I lay awake to listen to its roar,
and flowed with it, white-watering through dreams.
At daybreak, I could see it leaping still, baroque
and wild, its frothing whorled against some dark
idea. Then, lying back, I watched the mountains
move around the bowl of sky, its clouds immobile,
stained vermillion. The earth seemed secretive—

a mine, a trance, a single enigmatic fact sufficient
to itself, and we its aliens, restless, circling birds,
who cry, "How beautiful you look, how strange!"
We left that morning, breaking camp and heading
down toward Creede. I could not name the meaning
of the road, which snaked its way in the San Juans,
but felt a cool and unaccountable release, a lightness
as of river currents running into free, ecstatic thought.

On Prytania Street: Tending Lafayette Number 1

He pretends to be out walking—someone anonymous,
returning from the bank or CC's coffee bar,
or a tourist, alone; but his gait is stops and starts,
with furtive looks, half-turns and darting motions,
finally a sleight-of-hand, to find and extirpate
offending foliage—grasses, shoots of ivy,
miniature flowers—just a flash of color, an idea, yet
enough to crack a wall around the houses

of the dead. The cemetery gardens grow excessive,
cornucopias of green and red and yellow; but the grilles
have sunken like the mouths of toothless men;
the ancient skin of crypts is peeling, wrinkled
and discolored as a winter apple. Thought has dried
in there, the corpses shrunken in their crumbling
biers.—He sees me, picks up speed, but casts
an oblique glance at snaking fissures; pauses; sidles

over, brushing portions where the plaster is in pieces,
grabs a weed and jerks it outward by the roots,
then ambles innocently on—the dirt well shaken out
around the oaks, the plant now pocketed.
—We had a party once, among the tombs—neighbors
all, with sandwiches, a little band, some wine,
and ate and drank and talked while leaning
on the ancient monuments, our voices echoing

along the paths and through the emptiness. The filigree
of stone seemed light as air, and sculptures made
meringues; the angels, I remember, looked
as if they wished to smile, their lips about to part
in heavenly mirth.—The old man rounds the corner
towards Commander's Palace, pulls a pesky paw
of resurrection fern, and sashays back; the wall
has had its *toilette* for the day. Behind a screen—azalea,

oleander, pine—I watch him cross the street,
go up his steps, and shortly take his place behind
the glass in his *orangerie,* snipping a wayward leaf,
adjusting stakes, then gazing out as though
at children playing, chiding silently the antics
of the years—old green never disheartened, branches,
roots, the stubborn stalk; and old death too, there
always, gloating by the tombs, holding one for him.

In the Virgin Islands

I: Arriving

Roads in St. Thomas form a spider web, a giant
pretzel, rather, over-yeasted and irregular,
its center near Four Corners, where we'll stay
a week at the Viette estate. Jessie's come
to meet us at the airport in her Jeep, with Reggie
driving. It feels hot, all right, and moist—

a steam bath, like New Orleans. Hibiscus,
oleanders, palm trees, and a lazy pace—
it's all familiar. But the airport is the only flat spot
on the island, which still sees itself,
apparently, as a volcano. We rise at once, hit
hairpin curves, turn steeply, watch the roads

entangle with each other, then skein off.
It's left-side drive here, and we'll never
learn the routes: the maps are just approximate,
the numbers change or disappear.
I lean into a bend, feel branches brush the glass,
look up to catch a triangle of sky, look down

into a gully and a glimpse of rooftops, tiled
in red or blue. Discoursing on the weather,
Reggie claims it's been a tease all week—with haze
and showers in the mountains, St. John's
misty to the east, Tortola showing rarely,
and St. Croix invisible. All right: we'll not expect

a view, although the sky deceives us brilliantly.
Beyond a knot of roller-coaster roads,
we're on a jungle track, with jolts and gearbox
grindings; past a gate, another turn or so—
and suddenly we're parking at a platform
like a ferry landing, leading to the garden

and the house, which ride the cresting waves
of foliage, with palms and Norfolk Island pines
as masts. Ah, look between the trees!
Unblanched, without a veil or wisp of cloud,
the Caribbean Sea, as if at hand—a dazzling
mantle of blue moiré silk, with hems of turquoise,

green, aquamarine, and islet fasteners. We get
our luggage, take a few steps, and *voilà*:
there's the Atlantic, shimmering, a deeper
indigo. Did the day repent, knowing our visions
before we came? It's almost pain—the water's
body as if purposed for the moving mind.

II: In Jessie's Garden

Two hundred acres, with one hundred fifty kinds
of flowers, trees, and shrubbery; a single gardener,
her Reggie, calm, devoted, climbing up and down
the mountainside as if he were its lord—this might
be paradise. What curious birds are those that flash
among the foliage? What insects, crawling beasts;

what bursts of fire in the flamboyants—yellow, red—
the allamanda, scarlet bougainvillea; what desires
that shake the royal palms, or premises of death?
There in the chalices of a bromeliad, as new buds
open, rain dissolves the scattered ashes of a friend,
memorialized in green; and here is angel's trumpet,

ivory-pale, its fatal blossoms turning to the earth
in mourning. Jessie lives in exile, beyond tears,
remembering her daughters—fragile laughter, passing
grass—her husband stricken in the rose beds, calling
out for her above the blue illumination of the sea.
It would be better to be dead, she murmurs, gazing

out along the verdant terraces—to be a stone, or dust,
or frond of traveler's palm, which bends and sighs
and tatters in the wind—except for thinking those
who cannot think themselves, but wait, suspended
in their nothingness, on light and memory, and listen
as she draws them back toward being with her breath.

III: Reggie

Reggie wears two hats. Today—it's Sunday morning—
he has taken off his broadbrimmed gardener's
straw, and picks instead an old and shapeless
cotton thing, to drive us, as chauffeur,
to church in town. The Danes who settled here
bestowed their faith, their names, their architecture:

one imagines Luther as amazed from heaven
by the richly timbered vault, the formal rite,
the gothic windows opened onto palm trees tossing
in the wind as if the Spirit had descended
into them—bemused to hear the choir, dark as coal,
intone a Reformation hymn, then change

into a Caribbean band with shouts of "Hallelujah!"
and steel drums. Reggie, though, remains outside,
watching the Jeep or resting in the shade:
when pressed, he says that he believes in God,
but left the practice of his family, all dead
now, on Tortola—that communing in the trees,

the sun and rain, is good enough. I think of John
the Baptist in the wilderness, of bees and olive groves,
and wells where Christ athirst reposed,
and then Gethsemane—and how one dawn
an angel pointed in an empty tomb to bands of cloth
discarded on the stone, and Mary Magdalene,

distraught, supposed she saw the gardener,
a simple man of no pretensions, standing there alone;
and then she recognized her friend, and ran
to tell the others, who assumed that she was mad
with grief—announcing Eden reconciled
and green, the perishable body radiant, the earth reborn.

IV: Leaving

It's been too short; I'd like to draw out time
like a bungee cord and feel the island shouldering
the sky, or see its contours sway again
below the trees, at evening, when the sun
hoists scarlet sails and ploughs the ocean's edge,
turning up brass—or watch the bay, mercurial

with moonlight. But beauty here is merciless,
a sphinx, and will not travel. Well, these memories
are mine, at least, and portable. We've visited
St. John, had enchiladas there at dockside,
bathed in seven colors at Trunk Bay; we've written
postcards, sketched, and gone to Mountaintop,

the high point of St. Thomas, mooring Jessie's view;
with the tourists from the cruise ships,
we've combed the narrow streets to shop for jewels—
blue, green, amethyst, the water's eye;
we've ordered cocktails on the Hotel 1820 terrace,
and had dinner chez Hervé, next door,

as the old part of the city leaned into the darkness,
its lanterns bright as allamanda blooms.
We've talked with Reggie, gone to Megan's Bay,
the Legislature and the Frederick Church,
and lived a bit out of the world—the sort of interval
that makes one look up suddenly at the rest,

the thick quotidian, a sluggard thought slipping
into shadow. Things lie lightly now,
my gaze just glancing off, or glistening a moment,
spray on wings, as we depart; but the valences
have changed in us, a grave commotion
grounding passage, weighting the furtive world

In the Patio

What is our warrant here, beside
the bougainvillea, its blossoms of crepe paper
spilling everywhere—magenta, cantaloupe,
and pink? The lemon trees are hung
with fruit still green, like unlit lanterns; red
geraniums in the archway share a dry
perfume each time I pass. High up
on the patio wall, a hummingbird pursues

its own design through tangles
of a trumpet vine, winging in to drink
sweet nectar of the summer's end, a taste at every
flower, while a freshening wind meanders,
straying from the pristine drapery of sky.
The house, the whole of San Miguel
are cool, at least for me, ordinarily swathed
this season in Louisiana steam. As

we might expect, expressions of guitar
somewhere are manifest, running
over roofs, cascading down, so delicately
that they seem to emanate from nothingness.
For being here, I do not have
alas, the pretext of a need, a passion—
only a visitor, whose purpose
is to have none; for me this alien afternoon

has strange harmonics, as it were,
from other lives, or reveries of cloisters,
Oriental gardens, tapestries, as though I'd fallen
out of time, and into someone else's
painting, or a fantasy. It affords
the keenest sense of emptiness, a dizzying
lack of grounding, like the hours
of ocean crossings swinging on the bascule

of the waves. I feel things in their distance—
most of all myself, the light so just and generous
that textures all become a meaning
to be read, the shadows fill with depth,
and, past the trees, a pool of sky is eddying,
cerulean, profound, and borderless.
Oh, *amigos,* how beautiful the foreign is—
like you, the givers of what you may not possess.

Stars for Jubilee
January 2000

Well after dark, I walk up to the ninth-floor
deck, to watch ships on the river
shepherd in New Orleans for the night,
upstream, downstream, circling,
herding us in . . . Jewels sparkle in profusion:
emeralds, rubies, starboard
and port; amber lighting on the double

bridges; opal, sapphire, diamonds along
Canal Street, topaz on the dome,
and moonglow from the streetcars—all as if
in celebration, signaling to the skies.
It is so bright, the atmosphere
so clear, that I can read my watch,
or count the buttons on my blouse, and see

the humid air condensing on my wine glass,
forming drops, then channeling
like tears. Above, there should be heavenly
lamps; ah yes! That's Cassiopeia's
Chair? Aldebaran? and the Great Bear?
But they are pale, pale, receding
from my sight, as dreams are dissipated,

as our glittering years are gone. Where *are*
the stars? Only in our hearts, perhaps,
here in this late, electric world—
our brave and cordial hearts, our Janus hearts,
still beating through the darkness, claret
red, and calling toward sidereal
depths, keeping jubilee forever bright.

In the San Juans

The satisfaction, first, was to confound
the skeptics. We had stopped to talk with two—
a hirsute man from Texas, middle-aged,
beside a pickup truck, and then a younger chap,
his son, I guess, involved in struggles
with a motorcycle and a ramp. The parleying
took place just off the highway
at the entrance to a forest road we hoped

to take, ascending steeply from the Rio Grande.
By *we,* I mean five friends, three vehicles—
my Jeep, a monster diesel Ram
with an RV, and a Ford truck, well traveled,
towing a fifth wheel. The Texans had been up
off-road. "So what's it like up there?"
"It's mighty slippery . . . a mud-bowl, don't
you know. We managed to make out

on the two-wheeler, but I reckon that on four,
and pulling rigs like those, I wouldn't try.
Well, we'll be moseying on." The motorcycle
loaded on the back at last, the two
set off, and we consulted. Power we had,
big tires, and strong will; but it had rained—fat,
wholesome drops—on the San Juans
the day before. We drove up anyhow—

eight miles and more (I clocked it), gaining
height in spiral moves and grinding over rocks
and gravel. And the ruts were not too bad.
Though mire ruled out a likely spot
among some aspen, farther up where spruce
were thick, we found a loggers' track,
abandoned, which unraveled in a clearing
for a level camp. We had our water

with us. By evening, we had gathered wood,
laid out a ring of massive stones,
and built a fire that lasted seven hours.
Surrounded as we were by picket trees,
enclosed in folds of mountains, we surmised
the highest range off to the south, and felt
its shadows, as the sky, with Venus
barely visible, turned pale and powdery blue—

a lovely woman, but no longer young,
preferring softer lighting on her face,
and brilliants in her hair. So finally, the joy
was in ourselves. Beneath the fledgling
stars, we listened to the birds in evensong
and watched the smoke trail off
as from an offering, the old wood crackling
in the flames, the old hearts incandescent, pure.

On Her Sixty-Sixth Birthday

This measure is an artifice, and still,
old time surrounds me, running as it will,
the waters deeper now, the current slow,
but bearing my becoming in its flow.

A moment's pause, and what began as dream
inhabits its fulfillment in the stream:
the rocks and rough impressions disappear;
the rivulets are one; a bay is near;

and vast marine perspectives through the trees
propose lucidity and azure ease.
The motion steadies, and the world and I
meet in the pure gratuity of sky.